MW01249104

ISBN: 9798390514276

# Content

# INTRODUCTION

Success is not something achieved by chance. In reality, there is a proven formula used in all areas, from sports to business, to achieve great accomplishments. And it all begins with a simple belief: the Pygmalion effect. What is the Pygmalion effect, you may ask? It is the theory that our expectations of others can influence their behavior and, therefore, their performance. What is even more surprising is that this theory also applies to ourselves. If we learn to master the Pygmalion effect, we can take our life and career to the next level. In this book, you will discover how the Pygmalion effect will lead you to the top and how you can use this powerful tool to achieve your most ambitious goals. Get ready to discover the secret unveiled and transform your life forever.

# THE ORIGIN OF THE "PYGMALION EFFECT"

Once upon a time, there was a sculptor named Pygmalion who lived on a small Greek island. He was very talented and dedicated himself to creating beautiful marble statues. But despite being a highly recognized artist, Pygmalion felt lonely and sad because he had not found true love.

One day, he decided to sculpt a statue of a woman so beautiful and perfect that she seemed to be made of flesh and bone. He spent many days working on it, caring for every detail to make it perfect. And when he finally finished his masterpiece, he fell in love with it. He called her Galatea and treated her with such tenderness that he came to think she was a real person.

But Pygmalion was sad because his beloved statue could not reciprocate his love. So, one day, he visited the temple of Aphrodite, the goddess of love, and asked her to give him a wife like his statue. Aphrodite, moved by the sculptor's love and dedication, granted his request and gave life to the statue.

Upon returning home, Pygmalion touched the statue with his hand and was surprised to feel its warm and soft skin. Galatea had come to life and became his wife. They lived happily together, and their love was immortalized in legend.

While the myth of Pygmalion is one of the oldest stories about the power of belief, the modern theory of the Pygmalion Effect was not developed until the 1960s. In 1968, psychologist Robert Rosenthal and educator Lenore Jacobson conducted an experiment in a California elementary school that would forever change our understanding of the impact of expectations.

In the experiment, the researchers administered an intelligence test to all the students in the school and then informed the teachers that some of their students had obtained exceptional results. However, these students had not been selected based on their actual ability; the researchers had chosen the students at random. The teachers were unaware of this and instead believed that these students were the brightest in the class.

At the end of the school year, the students who had been identified as "smarter" achieved higher grades than their classmates, even though they had not demonstrated superior ability at the beginning of the school year. The mere fact that their teachers believed they were more capable and talented was enough for these students to excel. This pioneering study demonstrated that expectations can be a powerful tool for success or failure and laid the groundwork for the modern theory of the Pygmalion Effect. Since then, numerous studies have confirmed that expectations can influence performance in a wide variety of environments, from sports to education and work.

So, can we say that it is not about "miracles"? Correct, the Pygmalion Effect is not about a supernatural miracle or a magical force that suddenly makes things happen. Instead, it is based on the idea that our beliefs and expectations can influence our behavior and the behavior of others, which in turn can affect the outcome of the situations in which we find ourselves. By understanding and effectively using the Pygmalion Effect, we can improve our skills, performance, and results.

# HOW DOES THE PYGMALION EFFECT WORK IN OUR BODY?

The Pygmalion effect is related to the reticular activating system (RAS) which is a neuronal activation system located in the lower brainstem that filters and selects the information that reaches the brain.

This system functions as a filter that prioritizes information it deems important and relevant to us. When we have an expectation or belief about something, the RAS filters the information that aligns with that expectation and makes us more aware of it.

In the case of the Pygmalion effect, our expectations of another person can activate the RAS and make us pay more attention to behaviors that confirm those expectations. For example, if we expect a person to be a good leader, we are more likely to pay attention to behaviors that confirm that expectation and ignore or minimize behaviors that do not.

Some everyday examples of how the reticular activating system can influence our daily life:

When choosing a car: if we are looking to buy a particular car model, we are more likely to notice and pay attention to positive ads, articles, and comments that confirm our expectations about that model. This is because the RAS filters the information it receives to match our beliefs and expectations.

When choosing a diet: if we are looking to lose weight and believe that a particular diet is effective, we are more likely to pay attention to success stories and testimonials from people who have followed that diet. The RAS filters the information we receive and makes us more aware of behaviors that confirm our beliefs and expectations.

When choosing a career: if we have a clear idea of what we want to do in life, we are more likely to pay attention to job ads, news, and articles related to that career. The RAS filters the information we receive and makes us more aware of behaviors that confirm our beliefs and expectations about that particular career.

In summary, the reticular activating system helps us filter and select information that is relevant to us, based on our beliefs and expectations. This makes us more aware of behaviors that confirm our beliefs and expectations, which can influence our decisions and actions in daily life.

# WHO KNOWS ABOUT THE PYGMALION EFFECT AND BENEFITS FROM IT?

It's possible that many social networks use the information they have about us to validate our beliefs and expectations, although this hasn't been officially confirmed. It's known that social networks collect a large amount of information about our interests, behaviors, and preferences. This allows them to personalize the information they show us and adapt it to our individual needs and preferences.

In addition, social media algorithms are designed to show content that attracts our attention and generates engagement, as this allows them to keep us active on the platform and increase their retention time. This type of customization and adaptation of the information we receive on social media may be influenced by the reticular activating system.

In fact, some technology experts believe that social media algorithms are designed to validate our beliefs and keep us trapped in an echo chamber, where we only see and hear information that confirms our opinions and perspectives. However, it's important to note that the information we receive on social media isn't necessarily accurate or reliable and can be filtered to manipulate our opinions and decisions.

Therefore, it's important to be aware of how we use social media and seek alternative and varied sources of information to obtain a broader and more objective view of the topics that interest us. Similarly, it's important to note that social media isn't the only one that can use the reticular activating system to influence our expectations and behaviors.

Advertising and marketing can also use similar techniques to manipulate our perceptions and expectations about a product or service. For example, if a sportswear brand launches an advertising campaign that presents successful athletes using their products, this can increase our expectations about the quality and performance of that brand's sportswear.

If we already have a positive opinion about the brand, this can reinforce our positive expectations and motivate us to buy more products from that brand. On the other hand, if a fast-food brand launches an advertising campaign that presents happy and healthy people eating their products, this can increase our expectations about the quality and healthiness of that brand's food.

If we already have a positive opinion about the brand, this can reinforce our positive expectations and motivate us to buy more products from that brand. In summary, the reticular activating system and the Pygmalion effect can be used positively or negatively, depending on how they are used.

It's important to be aware of these techniques and use them ethically and responsibly to achieve our personal and professional goals. With all of the above, it's enough for you to realize that if others have always used it for their benefit and it has worked so far, there's nothing or no one stopping you from using the Pygmalion effect to get everything you want and propose in life.

# TECHNIQUES ON HOW TO USE THE PYGMALION EFFECT TO OUR ADVANTAGE

The Pygmalion Effect is a powerful tool that can help us achieve our goals and objectives in life. Here are some techniques to use this effect to our advantage:

1. Establish clear and specific goals: The first thing we need to do is have a clear and specific goal in mind. This goal should be something we really want to achieve and that aligns with our values and principles. Once we have this goal in mind, we must visualize ourselves achieving it and focus on it every day.

2. Create positive expectations: The expectations we have about ourselves and others can influence our behavior and performance. Therefore, it is important to have positive and realistic expectations about ourselves and others. If we believe we can achieve something, it is more likely that we will make it happen.

3. Use visualization: Visualization is a powerful technique that can help us achieve our goals. To use this technique, we must close our eyes and imagine ourselves achieving our goal. We must visualize every detail and feel the emotion of having achieved it. Visualization helps us believe in ourselves and increase our expectations of what we can achieve.

4. Communicate your expectations: Communication is key to using the Pygmalion Effect to our advantage. If we tell someone that we believe in them and expect great things from them, they are more likely to work hard and do their best to meet our expectations. Similarly, if someone tells us they believe in us and expect great things from us, we are more likely to work hard and do our best to meet those expectations.

5. Surround yourself with positive people: The people we surround ourselves with can influence our behavior and performance. Therefore, it is important to surround ourselves with positive people who support us and encourage us to achieve our goals. These people will help us maintain a positive and motivated attitude.

6. Celebrate your achievements: Finally, it is important to celebrate our achievements and successes. This will help us stay motivated and continue working hard to achieve our goals. Additionally, celebrating our achievements will help us increase our expectations of what we can achieve in the future.

Now, some practical examples: If your financial goal is to save enough money to buy a house in five years, you can apply some of these techniques. You can visualize what your dream home will look like and how it will feel when you finally buy it. You can look for role models, such as friends or family members who have achieved similar financial goals, and learn from their strategies. You can maintain a positive attitude and focus on taking positive steps to achieve your goal. And you can learn about personal finance and take calculated risks by investing your money in options that may increase your wealth in the long term.

1. Set specific and realistic goals: Defining clear and achievable goals is the first step to harnessing the power of the Pygmalion effect in financial success. Make sure to set goals that are specific, measurable, and realistic. For example, instead of saying "I want to be rich," define a more concrete goal like "I want to save 20% of my monthly income and grow my wealth by 5% each year."

2. Use visualization: Visualization is a powerful tool for achieving financial success. Visualize your future financial success and what you will do with your money. Imagine what your life will be like and how you will feel when you have achieved your goals. The more vivid your visualizations, the more likely you will be motivated and work hard to achieve them.

3. Believe in yourself: Belief in oneself is a crucial part of financial success. If you don't believe you can achieve your financial goals, then you probably won't. Believe in your ability to make smart financial decisions and have faith that you can achieve financial success.

4. Look for role models: Look for successful people in the financial field and observe what they do. Read about their success stories and learn from their financial strategies. By studying the experiences of others, you can discover useful techniques and tips to apply in your own life.

5. Maintain a positive attitude: Maintaining a positive attitude is key to achieving financial success. Learn to be optimistic and focus on solutions rather than problems. Focus on what you can control and take positive steps to reach your financial goals.

6. Learn about personal finance: Knowledge is power, especially in the financial world. Learn about personal finance, investments, savings, etc. By acquiring financial knowledge, you will be better prepared to make informed and strategic decisions that will lead you to financial success.
7. Learn to take calculated risks: Financial success often involves taking risks, but not all risks are equal. Learn to take calculated risks and do your due diligence before making important financial decisions. Don't be afraid to take risks, but make sure you are well-informed and prepared before doing so.

Another example, if you want to become the best writer in your field, you can seek out the most successful authors in your genre and read their works. Set specific goals, such as writing a certain number of words per day or completing a chapter every week. Visualize your success as a successful writer and maintain a positive mindset. Dedicate time to practicing your writing and seek out a mentor or coach who can offer you advice and guidance. Celebrate every achievement along the way and use that positive energy to stay motivated to keep advancing in your writing career.

Here are some specific techniques for becoming the best in a specific area using the Pygmalion effect:

1. Learn from the best: Seek out people who are the best in your field and learn from them. Whether it's a mentor, a book, an online course, or a conference, do your best to learn from people who have already achieved success in your area.

2. Set specific goals: It's important to have a clear idea of what you want to achieve and set specific goals to achieve it. Set realistic objectives and work towards them consistently.

3. Visualize success: Use visualization techniques to visualize yourself being successful in your area. Imagine every detail of your success, from how it feels to what you are doing at that moment. This can help strengthen your belief in yourself and increase your motivation to work hard to achieve your goal.

4. Maintain a positive mindset: Maintaining a positive and focused attitude is key to success in any area. Avoid distractions and negative influences and focus on your goal.

5. Practice, practice, practice: Consistent practice is crucial to becoming the best at anything. Dedicate time to practicing and perfecting your skills, and don't be afraid to make mistakes along the way.

6. Find a mentor or coach: A mentor or coach can help you stay motivated and focused on your goals. Seek out someone who has experience in your area and can offer you helpful guidance and advice.

7. Celebrate your successes: Every time you reach a goal or achieve a milestone, celebrate your success and use that positive energy to motivate yourself to keep working towards your next goal.

As you repeat affirmations and visualize your goals with emotion and detail, you are sending constant signals to your subconscious mind that those goals are important to you and that you desire them. Over time, your subconscious mind will begin to work in harmony with your conscious desires and seek out opportunities to help you achieve those goals. You may also notice that you become more aware of opportunities and resources available that can help you reach your objectives.

Additionally, using the Pygmalion Effect can also help you overcome your fears and limiting beliefs. As you focus on your goals and work to achieve them, your mind will begin to believe that they are possible. This can help you overcome obstacles that once seemed impossible and give you the confidence and motivation to keep moving forward.

I will stop here, as this is a turning point that can determine whether the Pygmalion Effect will work with a very high probability.

# INCREASING THE EFFECTIVENESS OF THE PYGMALION EFFECT

It's likely that you have many limiting beliefs implanted in your mind of which you're not even aware - beliefs that you've unconsciously acquired since you were a child until now. Limiting beliefs are ideas or thoughts that we have about ourselves or the world around us that limit our potential and capacity to achieve our goals. These beliefs can have different origins and can develop throughout our entire lives. Some of the most common sources are:

1. Childhood experiences: Childhood experiences can be an important source of limiting beliefs. For example, if someone received constant criticism as a child, they may develop a belief that they are not good enough or capable.
2. Culture and society: Limiting beliefs can also come from the culture and society in which one grows up. For example, if the society in which someone lives has a widespread belief that wealth is something bad or dirty, a limiting belief about money and financial success may develop.
3. Education and media: Education and the media can be important sources of limiting beliefs. For example, if someone receives an education that doesn't encourage creativity or risk-taking, a limiting belief about their own ability to innovate or start a business may develop.
4. Personal experiences: Personal experiences throughout life can also be a source of limiting beliefs. For example, if someone had a bad experience starting a business, a limiting belief about failure or risk may develop.

15

Now to land and understand how these can affect in a specific area, let's exemplify in the financial field.

Some limiting beliefs that can prevent you from growing and achieving your goals are:

*"Money is the root of all evil"*: *This belief can lead you to think that money is something bad or dirty, which can unconsciously keep you away from opportunities to generate income or make you feel guilty or ashamed of financial success.*

*"I'm not good enough to make money"*: *This limiting belief can make you feel insecure about your abilities and capabilities to make money, which can lead to procrastination or settling for an insufficient income level.*

*"I can't afford to be financially successful"*: *This limiting belief can make you believe that financial success is out of your reach or that you don't deserve it. This can limit your ability to make proper financial decisions and take advantage of investment opportunities.*

*"Money doesn't buy happiness"*: *While it's true that money is not the only source of happiness, this limiting belief can make you underestimate the importance of money in achieving your financial and personal goals.*

*"I can't afford to lose money"*: *This limiting belief can make you avoid taking necessary financial risks to grow and achieve your goals. It's important to remember that risk is part of any investment, and learning how to manage it effectively is key to achieving financial success.*

It's important to identify and work on these limiting beliefs to overcome them and achieve your financial goals, but there are also limiting beliefs that hinder personal growth and have the opposite effect of what the Pygmalion effect should be.

*"I don't have control over my life":* *This belief can make you feel powerless in the face of the situations around you, which can prevent you from taking actions to change or improve your personal situation.*

*"I don't have the necessary talent or skills to change":* *Believing that you don't have the necessary skills or talents to change or grow personally can make you feel defeated or frustrated when faced with challenges.*

*"I don't deserve to have success or happiness":* *Believing that you don't deserve to have success or happiness can lead you to sabotage your own efforts and settle for a life that doesn't satisfy you.*

*"I can't change my way of being or thinking":* *Believing that you can't change certain aspects of your personality or thinking can limit your ability to develop and improve as a person.*

*"There's nothing new that I can learn":* *Believing that you already know everything you need to know can make you close yourself off to new ideas and experiences, which can prevent you from growing and evolving as a person.*

I could continue giving you examples of limiting beliefs that hinder your progress and success in any area you propose, but now that you have become aware of their existence, it is time for you to eliminate them from your subconscious and start modifying them in such a way that from now on you can achieve everything you set your mind to.

Don't worry, I've been through this too, and I know it's a process that's not easy (or maybe it is, but we use the Pygmalion effect incorrectly by thinking that changing is difficult), but it is possible, and it all depends on you, on whether you believe it can be done or not, it all depends on the decisions you make from now on, and I know that now that you know everything I told you, you can make the right decision.

An effective way to eliminate limiting beliefs is to challenge and question their validity. For example, if you believe that you are not intelligent enough to learn a new language, ask yourself if that belief is supported by concrete and objective facts. You may discover that you have no real evidence to support that belief and that it is only a self-imposed idea.

Once you have identified and challenged your limiting beliefs, it is important to replace them with more positive and constructive thoughts. You can practice daily affirmation of positive phrases that empower you and help you build a new belief about yourself. For example, instead of saying "I am too shy to speak in public," you can affirm "I have the ability to speak in public with confidence and effectiveness."

If you have the limiting belief that you are not smart enough to learn a new language, you can challenge this belief by taking language classes and focusing on your progress. You can read books in that language, watch movies without subtitles, and seek opportunities to speak with native speakers. By doing so, you can see your progress and realize that, in reality, you are capable of learning a new language.

If you have the limiting belief that you are not good enough to get a promotion at work, you can challenge this belief by seeking opportunities to take the initiative in projects and demonstrate your ability. You can ask for feedback from your superiors to know where you need to improve and focus on developing those skills. By doing so, you can prove to yourself that you are capable of growing and advancing in your career.

If you have the limiting belief that you are not attractive enough to have a satisfying romantic relationship, you can challenge this belief by working on your self-esteem and confidence. You can focus on your positive qualities, work on your appearance, and attend social events to meet new people. By doing so, you can attract people who are attracted to your confidence and self-assurance, instead of focusing on your supposed "imperfections".

Remember that challenging your limiting beliefs can be a difficult and sometimes uncomfortable process, but it is crucial to constantly modify them for the effective application of the Pygmalion Effect in your life.

If you manage to overcome your limiting beliefs and change your thoughts and expectations about yourself, you are more likely to apply the Pygmalion Effect effectively in your life. The Pygmalion Effect is a manifestation of the self-fulfilling prophecy, in which a person's expectations can influence the behavior of another person or even their own behavior.

If you have negative limiting beliefs about yourself, you may tend to act in ways that confirm them. For example, if you believe that you are bad at math, you may not try as hard in your math classes, which can lead to poor results. If, on the other hand, you change your thoughts and expectations about yourself and begin to believe that you can be good at math, you are more likely to try harder and succeed in that area.

Therefore, by overcoming your limiting beliefs, you are opening the door to the possibility of applying the Pygmalion effect in a positive way, by having higher and more positive expectations of yourself and others. The opposite of the Pygmalion effect is known as the "Golem effect." This effect refers to the negative belief that someone is incapable or inept and can therefore influence that person's behavior and performance negatively. Like the Pygmalion effect, the Golem effect is a manifestation of the self-fulfilling prophecy. If someone believes that you are incapable or inept, it is more likely that you will act in ways that confirm those beliefs, which can have a negative effect on your self-esteem, motivation, and overall performance. It is important to remember that both the Pygmalion effect and the Golem effect can have a significant impact on people's lives, and it is important to be aware of the expectations we have of ourselves and others, in order to apply them in a positive and constructive way.

Next, I will show you a chart that displays how some variables interact that affect the effectiveness of the Pygmalion effect.

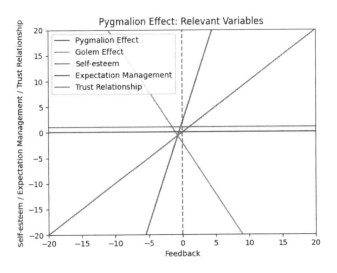

In the upper left quadrant (high self-esteem and low feedback), there is a situation where positive expectations are high, which can result in a Pygmalion effect, where the individual may have better performance and higher self-esteem. However, if feedback is low, this may not be enough to keep expectations and self-esteem high.

In the upper right quadrant (high self-esteem and high feedback), the individual has high expectations and high self-esteem, which can lead to a positive Pygmalion effect. High feedback can also help maintain high expectations and self-esteem.

In the lower right quadrant (low self-esteem and high feedback), the individual has low expectations and low self-esteem, which can result in a Golem effect, where the individual has poor performance and low self-esteem. However, if feedback is high, this can help increase self-esteem and improve performance.

In the lower left quadrant (low self-esteem and low feedback), the individual has low expectations and low self-esteem, which can lead to a negative Golem effect. Low feedback can also reinforce low expectations and low self-esteem.

Another tip to increase the effectiveness of the Pygmalion effect would be to use it on other people. The more people who believe in something, the more likely it is to manifest. For example, when others have high expectations for you, it can increase the effectiveness of the Pygmalion effect. This is because when someone else believes in you and has high expectations for your abilities, they are more likely to provide support and resources to help you achieve your goals. Additionally, it can be motivating to know that someone else has confidence in you, which can increase your self-esteem and motivation to work hard and achieve your objectives. However, it is important to remember that you should not rely completely on other people's expectations of you to achieve success. It is essential that you believe in yourself and your abilities so that you can make the most of the Pygmalion effect.

This is a secret that few know about and it is the origin of many "miracles." It would explain all those things that are impossible to happen, yet still happen. If a group of people believes something to be an absolute truth, they will do things accordingly without realizing it. Now that you understand this, I invite you to reflect on this phrase: "The sun doesn't rise every morning because it wants to, but because we want it to." This phrase can be interpreted in many ways, but since I learned how the Pygmalion effect works, I now understand it as suggesting that our beliefs and expectations can influence how we perceive and experience the world around us.

Now imagine that millions of people do this every day without realizing it. It makes me afraid to think that since the beginning of history, only a few have known how this effect works in all people, something that has perhaps benefited them in many ways. I invite you to reflect on this, whether it be in the form of ideologies, groups, or beliefs of all kinds. Now you know a secret that not everyone fully understands, as most media manipulations or mass controls of people (or even the direction the world is taking) are done with knowledge of how the Pygmalion effect works. It is up to you to decide how to act and think from now on and whether you want them to continue using the Pygmalion effect on you or decide to use it yourself to achieve everything you set out to do in life.

# ORIGIN OF THE "SELF-FULFILLING PROPHECY"

The term "self-fulfilling prophecy" was coined by sociologist Robert K. Merton in the 1940s. Merton observed that sometimes people's expectations about an event or behavior can influence its outcome. In other words, if someone believes that something will happen, it is more likely that person will act in a way that makes it happen, even if that belief is not based in reality. For example, if someone believes they are not good at math and expects to fail an exam, they may not study enough or put in enough effort, ultimately leading to failing the exam, thus fulfilling their own prophecy.

Some examples:

1.  The placebo effect: The placebo effect is a classic example of a self-fulfilling prophecy. When a person is given an inactive pill that they believe is medicine, they may experience a real improvement in their symptoms due to their belief in the power of the medicine. The belief in the pill's effectiveness itself becomes a self-fulfilling prophecy.

2.  Henry Ford's self-fulfilling prophecy: Henry Ford, the founder of Ford Motor Company, once said, "Whether you think you can or think you can't, you're right." He firmly believed in his own ability to innovate and lead in the automobile industry, and this belief led him to success. His belief became a self-fulfilling prophecy, as he worked hard and took risks to achieve his goals.

3. The success of the Beatles: In the early days of the Beatles, music critics considered them a mediocre and talentless band. However, their producer, George Martin, believed in them and encouraged them to keep working on their music. Martin gave them the opportunity to record their first single, "Love Me Do," and it became a surprising success. Martin's belief in the band became a self-fulfilling prophecy, as it gave them the confidence and momentum to keep working and improving their music, eventually leading them to become one of the most successful bands in music history.

Like the examples above, there are important milestones in history where the self-fulfilling prophecy has helped to materialize them. An example of this is the discovery of the periodic table. In the 19th century, chemists were looking for a way to organize all the known elements into a logical table. Russian chemist Dmitri Mendeleev was convinced that the periodic table existed and spent many years searching for it. His prophecy was that the elements could be ordered in a table according to their atomic weight and that elements with similar properties would be found in the same column.

To help organize information about chemical elements, Mendeleev started writing their properties on small cards and organized them into groups based on their chemical similarities. He then began playing with the cards, trying to find patterns and trends. As the story goes, one night he was working in his room and, after falling asleep, had a dream in which the chemical elements were arranged in a table.

When he woke up, he began working on the table just as he had seen it in his dream, and was able to successfully complete it.

Like Mendeleev, there are several examples of people who strongly believed in something and worked hard to make it happen, achieving incredible results. Some other examples are:

Roger Bannister: Bannister believed it was possible to run a mile in under four minutes, despite most experts believing it was physically impossible. He worked hard to train his body and mind, and in 1954, he broke the four-minute barrier by running a mile in 3 minutes and 59.4 seconds.

Thomas Edison: Edison believed he could find a way to create an electric light bulb that could last longer than previous ones. After thousands of attempts and failures, he finally found a carbon filament that lasted more than 1,200 hours, and the electric light bulb became a reality.

Stephen Hawking: Despite suffering from amyotrophic lateral sclerosis (ALS), a disease that eventually left him in a wheelchair and unable to speak, Hawking believed he could still make great contributions to theoretical physics. He worked tirelessly on his theory of black holes and became one of the most influential scientists of the 20th century.

J.K. Rowling: Rowling firmly believed in her idea of a series of books about a boy wizard named Harry Potter, even though she was rejected by several publishers before finding one willing to publish her work. With perseverance, success came and her book series became a global phenomenon.

In all these cases, these individuals had a strong belief in themselves and their ability to achieve their goals, and worked tirelessly to make those goals a reality. That's why I suggest that you do the same with yours, and I will also help you because I also believe that you can achieve anything you set your mind to (I am contributing to make that happen right now). Whoever you are, wherever you come from, I wrote this book because I know that this simple idea of understanding how the Pygmalion Effect works will change your life and how you live it forever.

# HOW TO CONTINUE LEARNING AND IMPROVING OUR KNOWLEDGE ABOUT THE PYGMALION EFFECT?

To continue learning and improving our knowledge about the Pygmalion effect, here are some recommendations:

1.  Read books and articles: There are numerous books and articles that discuss the Pygmalion effect and how to apply it in our lives. Some recommended titles are "The Pygmalion Effect" by Rosenthal and Jacobson, "The Self-Fulfilling Prophecy" by Robert K. Merton, and "Think Big" by David J. Schwartz.

2.  Participate in courses and workshops: There are courses and workshops that focus on personal development and how to apply the Pygmalion effect to achieve our goals. Research those that are available in your area.

3.  Observe others: Observe how successful people apply the Pygmalion effect in their lives. You can read their biographies, watch interviews or conferences, and take note of how they think and act to achieve what they want.

4.  Practice creative visualization: Creative visualization is a technique used to visualize our goals in detail, in order to attract them into our reality. By practicing it, we are applying the Pygmalion effect consciously.

5.  Ask for feedback: Ask trusted people to give you honest and constructive feedback about your performance and behavior. This will help you identify limiting beliefs and work on them.

Remember that knowledge about the Pygmalion effect is not enough to achieve our goals. It is necessary to apply it in our lives constantly and consciously, as well as learn how to bring out our full potential to accomplish anything we set our minds to.

In my personal opinion, I recommend learning skills to unleash your full potential, such as learning how to enter the "Flow State". The flow state is a term used in psychology to describe a mental state in which a person is completely immersed in an activity and feels fully absorbed by it. In this state, the person experiences a sense of deep concentration and loss of awareness of time. It is also described as a state of happiness or satisfaction.

The concept of flow was developed by psychologist Mihaly Csikszentmihalyi in the 1970s and has been widely researched and discussed since then. From a philosophical perspective, the flow state relates to the idea of self-transcendence, in which one transcends oneself and connects with something greater.

To develop your maximum potential, it is important to seek out activities that challenge you and allow you to enter the flow state. This can vary from person to person, but generally involves finding activities that combine challenge and skill at an optimal level. It is important to note that the flow state is not achieved simply by trying, but rather it is reached when working on an activity that fits your abilities and challenges.

Furthermore, the flow state also relates to the idea of mindfulness, in which one fully focuses on the present moment. By practicing mindfulness, you can improve your ability to enter the flow state and be more present in daily life, ultimately making it easier to achieve what you set out to do with the Pygmalion effect.

# HOW TO BOMBARD THE SUBCONSCIOUS TO ENHANCE THE PYGMALION EFFECT?

Now I will tell you some things that I do that have served me to constantly bombard my subconscious and modify my limiting beliefs, so that I am always in constant improvement and closer to my goals.

Identify the recurring things you do most in your day, for example, looking at your cellphone. Try changing your phone backgrounds to things that make you think you are always on the path towards your goals, but don't confuse this with putting a person as your background. It is recommended that you use inspiring images that remind you of your objective or what you want to happen, for example, an image of an athlete crossing the finish line in a race with the caption "never give up," or an image of the universe with the phrase "the sky is the limit."

A more specific example is if your Pygmalion Effect goals include being a famous and recognized writer, you could use an image of someone writing a book as your background, with inspiring quotes from well-known writers that motivate you to keep writing and pursuing your goal. This way, every time you see it, your subconscious will be more willing to show you or generate opportunities for you to achieve it. Be careful with this, as I mentioned in previous chapters, it may work negatively with images that do not relate to your goals.

Something similar would be to realize what you spend most of your time doing during the day, for example, on social media. In the case of Instagram, I recommend that you start following accounts related to what you want to achieve, whether they are motivational in the area you are seeking success in or have quality content that helps you or gives you ideas for opportunities to achieve your goal. The same can be done with Facebook, as its algorithm tries to show you more of what you like to see, so that you stay on the app longer. You should use this to your advantage, so that Facebook can work as a daily help to show you more related content and help you constantly grow in that area or topic.

In the case of WhatsApp, I recommend that you join groups related to people who are pursuing the same goal as you. This can help you meet people who are related to the same area and this will make more opportunities present themselves to you than before.

Now, in daily life, I know that most people do not live alone and it is inevitable not to run into people, whether they are family or friends, who have no idea about this topic and how harmful their limiting beliefs are, which they transmit to you just by spending time with them. I am not telling you to distance yourself from them or anything like that, but it is time for you to become aware of this and realize that every time you talk to people, they transmit their limiting beliefs to you, making you unconsciously accept them in your mind because there is an emotional and rational conflict within you (where the emotional generally wins, validating all the limiting beliefs of others).

In the previous case, there are 2 options. One is to distance yourself to avoid being contaminated by all these limiting beliefs that are told to you day by day, and the other is to realize every time you talk to them about all the limiting beliefs they are transmitting to you. You must deny them in your mind by telling yourself "that's a lie, those are their limiting beliefs", then you say a Denial of the limiting belief that was said and repeat it as part of yourself.

I know it's complex to see, so I'll give you some examples:

1.  If someone tells you "That's impossible to achieve", you can deny that limiting belief by telling yourself "Nothing is impossible, if I work hard and make an effort, I can achieve what I set out to do."

2.  If someone tells you "That career has no future, you should study something more secure", you can deny that limiting belief by telling yourself "I will not be influenced by the fears and limitations of others, I have the passion and skills to pursue my dreams."

3.  If someone tells you "You're too young/inexperienced for that", you can deny that limiting belief by telling yourself "Age and experience do not determine my ability to achieve what I want, I am willing to learn and grow on my path."

4.  If someone tells you "That's too difficult for you", you can deny that limiting belief by telling yourself "I will not allow the fear of failure to stop me, I am willing to face challenges and overcome them."

Remember that by denying these limiting beliefs, you are building a new, more positive and empowering mindset that will help you achieve your goals and objectives.

Shall I tell you something? When I told people that I would write a psychology book about success related to the Pygmalion Effect, they laughed sarcastically and told me to focus on studying or doing other things so as not to waste my time. It made me feel angry and frustrated, but I realized that I wouldn't gain anything by continuing to feel that way. So, I said to myself, "That's their limiting opinion, but I know that I have the potential and ability to write a successful book about the Pygmalion Effect that will help many people, just like it helped me. Their lack of belief won't affect me or stop me from reaching my goal." And look, I finally did it. In fact, the fact that they said that motivated me even more to complete the book because I realized that many people suffer from the same thing as me and need to know how to deal with it to truly achieve success in what they set out to do. It's important to focus on your own beliefs and not let other people's limiting beliefs affect you or stop you on your way to your goals.

Another way to help your subconscious provide you with opportunities for what you want is to avoid telling your goals or objectives to other people, including family, friends, or even your partner. Even if they say they support you, their limiting beliefs may make them not see your goals as real or view them negatively, and they may unconsciously take actions that prevent you from moving forward or achieving your goals (Golem effect). It's not their fault; it's the result of limiting beliefs that others have implanted in them throughout their lives. This is not always the case, but over time, you'll learn to distinguish how to do it. A more effective way is to make people understand that it's not something you want to achieve, but rather something that you're already achieving (in the present tense). If their subconscious accepts it as an absolute truth, they'll have no choice but to think and act with the belief that it's already happening, and everything they do will support your Pygmalion Effect.

Understand that this is not a "lie," as a lie is something that is not real, but this is something that is already manifesting through your actions and intentions, so it's real.

Please, I ask you from the bottom of my heart to be aware that the vast majority of people don't know that the Pygmalion Effect exists or how it works entirely, so be patient with them when you want to achieve everything you set out to do. The fact that you're here is not luck; you wanted it and unconsciously searched for it. It was something you needed to know for a long time, and now that you know it, you have no choice but to fulfill everything you want in life.